THE INSTANT
BUSINESS
FORMS BOOK

The Instant Business Forms Book
by Roger Pring

ISBN 0-517-10348-6

This 1994 edition published by Crescent
Books, distributed by Outlet Book Company,
Inc., a Random House Company,
40 Engelhard Avenue, Avenel, New Jersey
07001.

Printed in the United States of America.

1 2 3 4 5 6 7 8 9 10

THE INSTANT
BUSINESS
FORMS BOOK

by Roger Pring

CRESCENT BOOKS
New York • Avenel, New Jersey

CONTENTS

INTRODUCTION

EVERY YEAR IN THE U.S. hundreds of thousands of new businesses are started. And every year, thousands of small businesses fail. Studies by the Small Business Administration attribute the overwhelming majority of these failures to poor management. Unquestionably, sound management practices are crucial to the success of any business venture.

This book is designed to help you and your business. Every company, whether part time caterer or McDonald's, must keep efficient records if it is to succeed and grow. Well-organized records save your business time and money; help you stay abreast of customers, sales, inventories, cash flow; and keep you on top of the day-to-day operations of your business . . . they are, in short, the key to successful management.

In the following pages there are more than 200 forms, each designed for a specific purpose. Using the right form for the right job is not only easier and simpler, but it can make a customer respond more quickly to your invoice, or help a supplier fill an order promptly and accurately.

The four chapters are organized so that the forms you need are easy to find—simply look in the Table of Contents or the Index. All the forms have been perforated so that they can be removed easily, without tearing, and can be used over and over again.

Customizing the Forms

These forms have been designed to accommodate your company or organization letterhead. Once your logo is added to the master forms, you have a wide range of personalized stationery at your fingertips.

The simplest method of customizing the forms is to attach your business card in the space allotted on the master form; immediately you have customized forms in the exact quantity you require. To change the letterhead, simply change the business card. An alternative method is to use your company's rubber stamp on the master sheets. Make sure that the rubber stamp fits neatly into the space provided on the forms.

For the most professional-looking results, however, have your letterhead typeset or printed using presstype (available from most art supply stores) in the typeface of your choice and in a size and shape to fit on the master form. Then use this letterhead as your master in all your photocopying.

Recommendations for using form:

1. The area allowed for your imprint is 3⅜″ × 1¼″; on full-page forms; on half-page it is 3⅜″ × ¾″.

2. Those forms routinely mailed—invoices, statements, credit and debit memos, etc.—are designed so that the addressee's name will fit properly into a window envelope.

3. Many forms include extra space for information particular to your trade, e.g., delivery or handling charges on invoices,

union dues or profit sharing deductions on payroll forms.

4. By masking form entries that are unnecessary to your company, you can further customize any form. Liquid Paper® or white paper tape will be all you need.

5. If you choose to have the master forms reproduced by your local printer, you may want to inquire about having them padded in quantities of 25 or 50.

With **The Instant Business Forms Book,** you will always have the stationery you want, when you want it, and in the quantity you need. No more expensive printers' bills; no more being caught without; and no more having to store bulky boxes of forms.

INVOICE

Please send remittance to:

Sold to:

Shipping address:

Your account no: _____

Your order no: _____

Salesperson: _____

Invoice no: _____

Date: _____

Please refer to your account number and our invoice number in all communications regarding this invoice.

Shipped date: _____

Shipped via: _____

Qty ordered	Qty shipped	Item	Description	Unit price	Amount

PLEASE PAY THIS INVOICE; NO STATEMENT WILL BE SENT

SALES TAX _____

FREIGHT _____

TOTAL DUE

INVOICE

Please send remittance to:

Sold to:

Shipping address:

Qty ordered	Qty shipped	Item	Description	Unit price	Amount

PLEASE PAY THIS INVOICE;
NO STATEMENT WILL BE SENT

SALES TAX _____

FREIGHT _____

TOTAL DUE

Please refer to your account number and our invoice number in all communications regarding this invoice.

Your account no: _____

Your order no: _____

Salesperson: _____

Invoice no: _____

Date: _____

Shipping date: _____

Shipped via: _____

INVOICE

Please send remittance to:

Sold to:

Shipping address:

Qty ordered	Qty shipped	Item	Description	Unit price	Amount

PLEASE PAY THIS INVOICE;
NO STATEMENT WILL BE SENT

SALES TAX _____

FREIGHT _____

TOTAL DUE

Please refer to your account number and our invoice number in all communications regarding this invoice.

Your account no: _____

Your order no: _____

Salesperson: _____

Invoice no: _____

Date: _____

Shipping date: _____

Shipped via: _____

PRO FORMA INVOICE

Please send remittance to:

Sold to:

Shipping address:

Your account no:

Your order no:

Salesperson:

Invoice no:

Date:

Please refer to your account number and our invoice number in all communications regarding this invoice.

Qty ordered	Item	Description	Unit price	Amount

DUE ON RECEIPT OF THIS INVOICE;
SHIPMENT WILL BE MADE ON PAYMENT

SALES TAX _____

ESTIMATED
FREIGHT _____

TOTAL
DUE

INVOICE

Invoice no: _____

Date: _____

Customer name: _____

Address: _____

City: _____

State: _____   Zip: _____

Your order no: _____

Salesperson: _____

Shipped via: _____

Item	Quantity	Description	Unit price	Amount

PLEASE PAY BY INVOICE. NO STATEMENT WILL BE SENT.

TOTAL _____

BALANCE
DUE

THANK YOU FOR YOUR ORDER

INVOICE

Invoice no: _____

Date: _____

Customer name: _____

Address: _____

City: _____

State: _____   Zip: _____

Your order no: _____

Salesperson: _____

Shipped via: _____

Item	Quantity	Description	Unit price	Amount

PLEASE PAY BY INVOICE. NO STATEMENT WILL BE SENT.

TOTAL _____

BALANCE
DUE

THANK YOU FOR YOUR ORDER

SALES SLIP

Date:

Name: APT/FL:

Address: Telephone:

City: Business telephone:
State:
Zip:

Sold by   Cash   COD   Charge: MC/ V/ AE/ Other   On account

Quantity	Item	Price	Amount
1			
2			
3			
4			
5			
6			
7			

TOTAL

Received by: TOTAL DUE

ANY RETURN MUST BE
ACCOMPANIED BY THIS
SALES SLIP

SALES SLIP

Date:

Name: APT/FL:

Address: Telephone:

City: Business telephone:
State:
Zip:

Sold by   Cash   COD   Charge: MC/ V/ AE/ Other   On account

Quantity	Item	Price	Amount
1			
2			
3			
4			
5			
6			
7			

TOTAL

Received by: TOTAL DUE

ANY RETURN MUST BE
ACCOMPANIED BY THIS
SALES SLIP

Sold by: _____ Date: _____

Name: _____

Address: _____

_____ _____ _____
_____ _____ _____
_____ _____ _____
_____ _____ _____
_____ _____ _____
_____ _____ _____
_____ _____ _____
_____ _____ _____
_____ _____ _____

All returns and exchanges must   Total [   ]
be accompanied by this receipt

THANK YOU

Sold by: _____ Date: _____

Name: _____

Address: _____

_____ _____ _____
_____ _____ _____
_____ _____ _____
_____ _____ _____
_____ _____ _____
_____ _____ _____
_____ _____ _____
_____ _____ _____
_____ _____ _____

All returns and exchanges must   Total [   ]
be accompanied by this receipt

THANK YOU

Sold by: _____ Date: _____

Name: _____

Address: _____

_____ _____ _____
_____ _____ _____
_____ _____ _____
_____ _____ _____
_____ _____ _____
_____ _____ _____
_____ _____ _____
_____ _____ _____
_____ _____ _____

All returns and exchanges must   Total [   ]
be accompanied by this receipt

THANK YOU

Sold by: _____ Date: _____

Name: _____

Address: _____

_____ _____ _____
_____ _____ _____
_____ _____ _____
_____ _____ _____
_____ _____ _____
_____ _____ _____
_____ _____ _____
_____ _____ _____
_____ _____ _____

All returns and exchanges must   Total [   ]
be accompanied by this receipt

THANK YOU

CALL NOTICE

Name:

Address:

Record no:

We were here on _____ at _____

Please call _____ to arrange another

appointment.

CALL NOTICE

Name:

Address:

Record no:

We were here on _____ at _____

Please call _____ to arrange another

appointment.

CALL NOTICE

Name:

Address:

Record no:

We were here on _____ at _____

Please call _____ to arrange another

appointment.

CALL NOTICE

Name:

Address:

Record no:

We were here on _____ at _____

Please call _____ to arrange another

appointment.

DELIVERY SLIP

Delivery no:

Date:

Requisition/
order no:

Delivered to:

The following received in good order:

Quantity	Number	Description

Signed:

DELIVERY SLIP

Delivery no:

Date:

Requisition/
order no:

Delivered to:

The following received in good order:

Quantity	Number	Description

Signed:

LAYAWAY FORM

Date:

Salesperson:

☐ To be picked up

☐ Delivered

Sold to:

Item/Description	Quantity	Unit price	Amount

PAYMENT PLAN		payments
$		each
$		final payment

Date	Amount due	Payment

TOTAL

SALES TAX

TOTAL DUE

DEPOSIT

BALANCE

LAYAWAY FORM

Date:

Salesperson:

☐ To be picked up

☐ Delivered

Sold to:

Item/Description	Quantity	Unit price	Amount

PAYMENT PLAN		payments
$		each
$		final payment

Date	Amount due	Payment

TOTAL

SALES TAX

TOTAL DUE

DEPOSIT

BALANCE

STATEMENT

Date:

In account with:

Date:		Amount
	Previous balance	
	Payment received	

PLEASE PAY THIS AMOUNT

STATEMENT

Date:

In account with:

Date	Amount
Previous balance	
Payment received	

PLEASE PAY THIS AMOUNT

STATEMENT

Date:

In account with:

Date	Amount
Previous balance	
Payment received	

PLEASE PAY THIS AMOUNT

THE INSTANT BUSINESS FORMS BOOK

SALES ORDER FOR DELIVERY

Date:

Salesperson:

Ship via:

Name: APT/FL:

Address: Telephone:

City: Business telephone:
State:
Zip:

Qty ordered	Description	Shipped	Unit price	Amount
			SUB TOTAL	

Terms:

Received by: TOTAL

SALES ORDER FOR DELIVERY

Date:

Salesperson:

Ship via:

Name: APT/FL:

Address: Telephone:

City: Business telephone:
State:
Zip:

Qty ordered	Description	Shipped	Unit price	Amount
			SUB TOTAL	

Terms:

Received by: TOTAL

ORDER FORM

Order no: _____

Date: _____

Salesperson: _____

Sold to:

Shipping address:

Telephone: _____

Ship via: _____

Date: _____

Quantity	Description	Unit price	Amount

TERMS:

☐ Cash

☐ COD

☐ On account

☐ Charge: MC/V/AE/Other

SUB TOTAL _____

SALES TAX _____

TOTAL _____

DELIVERY CHARGE _____

BALANCE DUE _____

ORDER FORM

Order no:

Date:

Salesperson:

Shipping address:

Sold to:

Telephone:

Ship via:

Date:

Quantity	Description	Unit price	Amount

SUB TOTAL

SALES TAX

TOTAL

DELIVERY

CHARGE

BALANCE DUE

TERMS:
- Cash
- COD
- On account
- Charge:
  MC/V/AE/Other

ORDER FORM

Order no:

Date:

Salesperson:

Shipping address:

Sold to:

Telephone:

Ship via:

Date:

Quantity	Description	Unit price	Amount

SUB TOTAL

SALES TAX

TOTAL

DELIVERY

CHARGE

BALANCE DUE

TERMS:
- Cash
- COD
- On account
- Charge:
  MC/V/AE/Other

TELEPHONE ORDER

Customer no:

Order no:

Delivery date:

Ship via:

Sold to:

Deliver to:

Item	Quantity ordered	Description	Quantity shipped	Quantity backordered	Unit price	Amount

SUB TOTAL

TOTAL

Payment terms:

Sales signature:

Date:

TELEPHONE ORDER

Customer no:

Order no:

Delivery date:

Ship via:

Sold to:

Deliver to:

Item	Quantity ordered	Description	Quantity shipped	Quantity backordered	Unit price	Amount

SUB TOTAL

Payment terms:

Sales signature:

Date:

TOTAL

TELEPHONE ORDER

Customer no:

Order no:

Delivery date:

Ship via:

Sold to:

Deliver to:

Item	Quantity ordered	Description	Quantity shipped	Quantity backordered	Unit price	Amount

SUB TOTAL

Payment terms:

Sales signature:

Date:

TOTAL

TELEPHONE ORDER

Order date: _____

Customer no: _____

Your order no: _____

Our order no: _____

Sold to: _____

City: _____
State: _____   Zip: _____
Attention: _____   Telephone: _____

Shipping address: _____

City: _____
State: _____   Zip: _____
Attention: _____   Telephone: _____

FOB: _____

Label: _____

No backorders ☐

Delivery date: _____

Shipping date: _____

Shipping route: _____

Quantity ordered	Item no.	Description	Quantity shipped	Quantity backordered	Unit price	Amount

Backorders will be shipped on or before: _____

SUB TOTAL

PAYMENT TERMS

TOTAL ☐

Salesperson: _____

Date: _____

SPECIAL ORDER

Date:

Delivery date:

Sold to:

City:

State: Zip:

Telephone:

Business telephone:

Sold by   Cash   COD   Charge: MC/V/AE/Other

Quantity	Description	Price	Amount

Size: Type:

Remarks:

DEPOSIT

BALANCE
DUE

Order taken by:

SPECIAL ORDER

Date:

Delivery date:

Sold to:

Telephone:

City:
State:
Zip:

Business telephone:

Sold by   Cash   COD   Charge: MC/V/AE/Other

Quantity	Description	Price	Amount

Size: Type:

Remarks:

DEPOSIT

BALANCE DUE

Order taken by:

SPECIAL ORDER

Date:

Delivery date:

Sold to:

Telephone:

City:
State:
Zip:

Business telephone:

Sold by   Cash   COD   Charge: MC/V/AE/Other

Quantity	Description	Price	Amount

Size: Type:

Remarks:

DEPOSIT

BALANCE DUE

Order taken by:

COMMERCIAL CREDIT APPLICATION

Trade name: _____   Address: _____

                                                  Telephone: _____

Name of accounts payable contact: _____   Title: _____

Approx. annual sales: _____   Year incorporated or registered: _____

Credit line requested: _____

☐ Corporation   ☐ Partnership   ☐ Individual

OWNERSHIP	Name: Title: % Ownership:	Address: Telephone:
	Name: Title: % Ownership:	Address: Telephone:
TRADE REFERENCES	Name: Contact name:	Address: Telephone:
	Name: Contact name:	Address: Telephone:
	Name: Contact name:	Address: Telephone:
BANK REFERENCES	Name: Office: Account no:	Address: Telephone:

In consideration for credit being extended, I or we acknowledge and agree to the following: (1) Payment is jointly, severally and unconditionally guaranteed within 30 days of date of delivery; (2) any charges unpaid after the above 30 days are to be increased by 1½% per month; (3) any charges still outstanding after 90 days from date of delivery are subject to collection, and all collection or arbitration expenses, attorneys' fees, and court costs will be borne by the purchaser; (4) title to all work shall remain with the creditor until all invoices and additional charges have been paid in full; (5) all claims, requests for adjustments, or notification of errors must be made within thirty days, or charges are considered accepted; (6) this agreement shall apply to all current and future charges unless revocation is received by registered mail; (7) credit privileges may be withdrawn at any time without invalidating the terms of this agreement.

CREDIT CANNOT BE EXTENDED UNTIL THIS FORM IS
COMPLETED AND VERIFIED

Authorized signature: _____

Title: _____

Date: _____

CREDIT APPLICATION

Name: Residence:

Spouse's name: City:
                                         State: Zip:

Telephone: Length of time
                                         at this address:

Previous address:
                                         City:
                                         State: Zip:

Employed by: Address:

Supervisor:
                                         City:
Telephone: State: Zip:

Position: Annual earnings:

Previous employer: Address:

Supervisor:
                                         City:
Telephone: State: Zip:

Position: Annual earnings:

Spouse employed by: Address:

Supervisor:
                                         City:
Telephone: State: Zip:

Position: Annual earnings:

Bank reference: Checking: Other income:

                   Savings:

Trade references: 1

                       2

                       3

CREDIT INQUIRY

Date: _____

To: ⌐   ¬
Address:

_____

                              TO PROCESS A CREDIT APPLICATION,
                              WE ASK YOU IN CONFIDENCE
⌐   ⌐ TO GIVE US THE FOLLOWING INFORMATION:

Applicant: Address:

                                              City:
                                              State: Zip:

Dollar sales this year: _____   Terms:

Last year: _____

Largest amount owed: _____

Prompt: ☐ Yes
            ☐ No

Amount now owed: _____   Payment
                                       pattern: ☐ Prompt
Current: ☐ Yes   ☐ Slow
            ☐ No   ☐ Very slow

☐ Credit extended   ☐ Refused
                        Please explain:

☐ Please check one   ☐ Prompt – satisfactory   ☐ Slow – collectible
                      ☐ Prompt – _____ days slow   ☐ Slow – uncollectible
                      ☐ Makes partial payment   ☐ To Attorney for collection

☐ Please check one   ☐ A good account –   ☐ We do not recommend
                        recommended   this account

FOR YOUR CONVENIENCE, WE ENCLOSE A STAMPED,   Name: _____
ADDRESSED ENVELOPE FOR REPLY.
WE WILL RECIPROCATE GIVING YOU INFORMATION   Telephone: _____
WE HAVE REGARDING CREDIT DECISIONS.
THANK YOU FOR YOUR HELP.

CREDIT HISTORY

Name: _____   Spouse: _____

Address: _____

Telephone: _____

Business address: _____   Business address: _____

Business telephone: _____   Business telephone: _____

Date approved	Credit line	Payment due		Payment received		Balance	Date notice sent	Date 2nd notice sent
		Amount	Date	Amount	Date			

Collection call: _____

Date to Attorney: _____

Disposition: _____

CREDIT HISTORY

Name:

Address:

Spouse: _____   Telephone: _____

Business address: _____   Business address: _____

Business telephone: _____   Business telephone: _____

Date approved	Credit line	Payment due Amount	Date	Payment received Amount	Date	Balance	Date notice sent	Date 2nd notice sent

Collection call: _____   Date to Attorney: _____   Disposition: _____

CREDIT HISTORY

Name:

Address:

Spouse: _____   Telephone: _____

Business address: _____   Business address: _____

Business telephone: _____   Business telephone: _____

Date approved	Credit line	Payment due Amount	Date	Payment received Amount	Date	Balance	Date notice sent	Date 2nd notice sent

Collection call: _____   Date to Attorney: _____   Disposition: _____

COLLECTION NOTICE

Date: _____

Account no: _____

To:

NOTICE OF PAYMENT PAST DUE

Amount due	Minimum payment due	Finance/Interest charges

PAYMENT MUST BE RECEIVED ON OR BEFORE: _____

TO DISCUSS YOUR ACCOUNT
PLEASE CONTACT DIRECTLY: _____

Name   Telephone

COLLECTION NOTICE

Date: _____

Account no: _____

┌ To: ┐

└   ┘ NOTICE OF PAYMENT PAST DUE

Amount due	Minimum payment due	Finance/Interest charges

PAYMENT MUST BE RECEIVED ON OR BEFORE: _____

TO DISCUSS YOUR ACCOUNT
PLEASE CONTACT DIRECTLY: _____

Name   Telephone

COLLECTION NOTICE

Date: _____

Account no: _____

┌ To: ┐

└   ┘ NOTICE OF PAYMENT PAST DUE

Amount due	Minimum payment due	Finance/Interest charges

PAYMENT MUST BE RECEIVED ON OR BEFORE: _____

TO DISCUSS YOUR ACCOUNT
PLEASE CONTACT DIRECTLY: _____

Name   Telephone

SAMPLE REQUEST

Date:

Name: Title: Address:

Company: Telephone:
                                                    City:
                                                    State: Zip:

☐ New account   ☐ Previous customer   ☐ Charge   ☐ No charge

Quantity	Description	Total

Ship via:

Notify:

Signed:

Authorized:

CREDIT LIST

Period from: _____

to: _____

Account number	Account name	Date opened	Credit line	Credit available	Credit used	Current	30	60	90

TOTALS

RETURNED CHECK NOTICE

Date:

Your check no:

Amount:

Date of check:

Bank:

Branch:

Your check has been returned unpaid. Please contact us immediately to arrange payment.

Signed:

RETURNED CHECK NOTICE

Date:

Your check no:

Amount:

Date of check:

Bank:

Branch:

Your check has been returned unpaid. Please contact us immediately to arrange payment.

Signed:

CUSTOMER RETURN/EXCHANGE

Date:

From:

Telephone:

Address:

City:
State: Zip:

Quantity	Description	Price	Amount

☐ Exchange

☐ Credit

☐ Cash

☐ Check

☐ Charge: MC/ V/ AE/ Other

Date sold:

Reason for return:

Signed:

RETURN AUTHORIZATION

Return authorization no: _____

Customer no: _____

Return date: _____

Sold to:

Return to:

Attn:

Attn:

Shipped to:

Your order no: _____

Order date: _____

Attn:

Our order no: _____

Item	Qty shipped	Description	Qty received	Unit price	Amount

TOTAL [_____]

☐ No credit to be issued; will be reshipped

☐ Credit to be issued in the amount of: $ _____

Reason for return: _____

Date: _____

Approved by: _____

CREDIT MEMO

Date issued: _____

Customer no: _____

Your order no: _____

Dated: _____

To:

Shipping address:

GOODS RETURNED   Date received: _____

Quantity	Item/no.	Unit price	Amount	Reason for credit

Notes:

TOTAL CREDIT

Approved by: _____

Date: _____

Approved by: _____

Date: _____

CREDIT MEMO

Date issued:

Customer no:

Your order no:

Dated:

To:

Shipping address:

GOODS RETURNED			Date received:		
Quantity	Item/no.	Unit price	Amount		Reason for credit

TOTAL CREDIT

Notes:

Approved by:

Date:

Approved by:

Date:

CREDIT MEMO

Date issued:

Customer no:

Your order no:

Dated:

To:

Shipping address:

GOODS RETURNED			Date received:		
Quantity	Item/no.	Unit price	Amount		Reason for credit

TOTAL CREDIT

Notes:

Approved by:

Date:

Approved by:

Date:

DEBIT MEMO

Date issued: _____

Customer no: _____

Your order no: _____

Dated: _____

To:

Shipping address:

Quantity	Item/no.	Unit price	Amount	Reason for debit

Notes:

TOTAL DEBIT _____

Approved by: _____

Date: _____

Approved by: _____

Date: _____

DEBIT MEMO

Date issued:

Customer no:

Your order no:

Dated:

Shipping address:

To:

Quantity	Item/no.	Unit price	Amount	Reason for debit

TOTAL DEBIT

Notes:

Approved by:

Date:

Approved by:

Date:

DEBIT MEMO

Date issued:

Customer no:

Your order no:

Dated:

Shipping address:

To:

Quantity	Item/no.	Unit price	Amount	Reason for debit

TOTAL DEBIT

Notes:

Approved by:

Date:

Approved by:

Date:

BACKORDER REPORT

Period from:

to:

Item number	Description	Quantity on order	Quantity back-ordered	TOTAL	Date ordered	Due	Received

Signed:

BACKORDER REPORT

Period from:

to:

Item number	Description	Quantity on order	Quantity back-ordered	TOTAL	Date ordered	Due	Received

Signed:

BACKORDER REPORT

Period from:

to:

Item number	Description	Quantity on order	Quantity back-ordered	TOTAL	Date ordered	Due	Received

Signed:

DAILY SALES CALL REPORT

Date:

Page ___ of ___

Sales: _____

Address: _____

Product line: _____ Territory: _____

City:
State: _____ Zip: _____

Firm name/Address	Person contacted/Title	Result	$ Sold	Follow-up

TOTAL
SALES [   ]

TOTAL
CALLS [   ]

Signature: _____

WEEKLY SALES CALL REPORT

Date: _____

Period from: _____

to: _____

Page _____ of _____

Sales: _____

Address: _____

Product line: _____   Territory: _____

City: _____

State: _____   Zip: _____

Firm name/Address	Person contacted/Title	Result	$ Sold	Follow-up

TOTAL SALES [   ]

TOTAL CALLS [   ]

_____
Signature:

TELEPHONE SALES REPORT

Date:

Period:

Page   of

Sales:

Address:

Product line: Territory:

City:
State: Zip:

Firm name/Address/ Telephone	Party contacted/Title	Result	$ Sold	Follow-up

TOTAL
SALES

TOTAL
CALLS

Signature:

SALES FOLLOW-UP

Date: _____

Period from: _____

to: _____

Salesperson: _____

Territory: _____

		Date last contact	Proposal	Result	Follow-up
Customer:					
Address:					
Telephone:					
Contact:					
Customer:					
Address:					
Telephone:					
Contact:					
Customer:					
Address:					
Telephone:					
Contact:					
Customer:					
Address:					
Telephone:					
Contact:					

SALES FOLLOW-UP

Name:

Telephone:

Address:

Type of business:

Contact:

Title:

Initial contact:

Interest in:

Proposal:

Date	Report of call	Follow-up	Initials

SALES FOLLOW-UP

Name:

Telephone:

Address:

Type of business:

Contact:

Title:

Initial contact:

Interest in:

Proposal:

Date	Report of call	Follow-up	Initials

SALES FOLLOW-UP 47

GROSS PROFIT, ITEMIZED

Period from:

to:

GROSS PROFIT, ITEMIZED

Item	Supplier	Quantity ordered	Unit cost	Unit selling price	Gross profit by unit	% Profit to selling price

Signed:

DISCOUNT SCHEDULE

☐ Retail

☐ Wholesale

Item	Retail price	Quantity	% — Amount of discount	Net unit price

Valid from:

to:

COMMISSION STATEMENT

Name:

Period from:

to:

Order date	Order number	Account	Invoice amount	Commission Rate	Amount

TOTAL
SALES

TOTAL
COMMISSION
EARNED

LESS
ADVANCE/
CREDIT

COMMISSION
PAYABLE

Signed:

Date:

COMMISSION STATEMENT

Name:

Period from:

to:

Order date	Order number	Account	Invoice amount	Commission Rate	Amount

TOTAL SALES

TOTAL COMMISSION EARNED

LESS ADVANCE/CREDIT

COMMISSION PAYABLE

Signed:

Date:

COMMISSION STATEMENT

Name:

Period from:

to:

Order date	Order number	Account	Invoice amount	Commission Rate	Amount

TOTAL SALES

TOTAL COMMISSION EARNED

LESS ADVANCE/CREDIT

COMMISSION PAYABLE

Signed:

Date:

DAILY CASH REPORT

Date: _____

CASH PAID TO:

	Name	$
1		
2		
3		
4		
5		
6		
7		
8		
9		
10		

TOTAL ITEMS _____ **TOTAL $** _____

CHECKS PAID TO:

	Name	$
1		
2		
3		
4		
5		
6		
7		
8		
9		
10		

TOTAL ITEMS _____ **TOTAL $** _____

RECEIPTS FROM:

	Name	$
1		
2		
3		
4		
5		
6		
7		
8		
9		
10		

TOTAL RECEIPTS [   ]

LESS CASH PAID OUT _____

ADD CASH FUND _____

BALANCE [   ]

OVER _____

SHORT _____

BANK DEPOSIT [   ]

Deposit no: _____

Deposit date: _____

Deposit made by: _____

Signed: _____

Report date: _____

Comments: _____

DAILY CASH REPORT

Date: _____

CASH PAID TO:			CHECKS PAID TO:			RECEIPTS FROM:	
	Name	$		Name	$		Name	$
1			1			1	
2			2			2	
3			3			3	
4			4			4	
5			5			5	
6			6			6	
7			7			7	
8			8			8	
9			9			9	
10			10			10	

TOTAL ITEMS	TOTAL $		TOTAL ITEMS	TOTAL $

TOTAL RECEIPTS _____

LESS CASH PAID OUT _____

ADD CASH FUND _____

BALANCE _____

OVER _____

SHORT _____

BANK DEPOSIT _____

Comments: _____

Deposit no: _____ Deposit date: _____ Deposit made by: _____

Signed: _____ Report date: _____

DAILY CASH REPORT

Date: _____

CASH PAID TO:			CHECKS PAID TO:			RECEIPTS FROM:	
	Name	$		Name	$		Name	$
1			1			1	
2			2			2	
3			3			3	
4			4			4	
5			5			5	
6			6			6	
7			7			7	
8			8			8	
9			9			9	
10			10			10	

TOTAL ITEMS	TOTAL $		TOTAL ITEMS	TOTAL $

TOTAL RECEIPTS _____

LESS CASH PAID OUT _____

ADD CASH FUND _____

BALANCE _____

OVER _____

SHORT _____

BANK DEPOSIT _____

Comments: _____

Deposit no: _____ Deposit date: _____ Deposit made by: _____

Signed: _____ Report date: _____

CASHIER'S BALANCE SLIP

Name:

Department:

Register no:

Date:

Time:

Amount of
change bank:

DENOMINATION	Amount in	Amount out
Pennies		
Nickels		
Dimes		
Quarters		
Halves		
Dollars		
Fives		
Tens		
Twenties		
Fifties		
Hundreds		
TOTAL		

Signed:

CASHIER'S BALANCE SLIP

Name:

Department:

Register no:

Date:

Time:

Amount of
change bank:

DENOMINATION	Amount in	Amount out
Pennies		
Nickels		
Dimes		
Quarters		
Halves		
Dollars		
Fives		
Tens		
Twenties		
Fifties		
Hundreds		
TOTAL		

Signed:

	Date added to list	Customer number	Name	Address	Mailing sent	Maintain	Drop
1							
2							
3							
4							
5							
6							
7							
8							
9							
10							
11							
12							
13							
14							
15							
16							
17							
18							
19							
20							
21							
22							
23							
24							

MEETING AGENDA

Function: _____

Location: _____

Date: _____

Attending: _____

Time	
8:00 – 8:30	
8:30 – 9:00	
9:00 – 9:30	
9:30 – 10:00	
10:00 – 10:30	
10:30 – 11:00	
11:00 – 11:30	
11:30 – 12:00	
12:00 – 12:30	
12:30 – 1:00	
1:00 – 1:30	
1:30 – 2:00	
2:00 – 2:30	
2:30 – 3:00	
3:00 – 3:30	
3:30 – 4:00	
4:00 – 4:30	
4:30 – 5:00	
5:00 – 5:30	
5:30 – 6:00	
6:00 – 6:30	
6:30 – 7:00	
7:00 – 7:30	
7:30 – 8:00	
8:00 – 8:30	
8:30 – 9:00	

JOURNAL ENTRIES

Number: _____

Month of: _____ 19 ___

CHARGES				DATE	DESCRIPTION	CREDITS			
ACCOUNTS RECEIVABLE	ACCOUNTS PAYABLE	GENERAL LEDGER				GENERAL LEDGER		ACCOUNTS PAYABLE	ACCOUNTS RECEIVABLE
		Acct. no.	Amount			Acct. no.	Amount		
					Amount brought forward				

GENERAL LEDGER

Account number: _____

Account name: _____

Address: _____

Sheet: _____ of _____

DATE	DESCRIPTION	CHARGES	CREDITS	BALANCE
	Amount brought forward			

GENERAL LEDGER

Account number:

Account name:

Address:

Sheet: _____ of _____

DATE	DESCRIPTION	CHARGES	CREDITS	BALANCE	
				Charges	Credits
	Amount brought forward				

DISTRIBUTION OF INVOICES

Month of: _____ 19 ___

Sheet: ___ of ___

DATE OF INVOICE	INVOICE NUMBER	CREDIT ACCOUNTS PAYABLE	DESCRIPTION	GENERAL ACCOUNTS		DATE PAID	CHECK NUMBER
				Name of account	Amount		
			Amount forwarded				

STOCK LEDGER

Unit: _____
Article: _____
Minimum: _____
Location: _____

DATE	DESCRIPTION	RECEIVED			DISBURSED		BALANCE ON HAND	
		Quantity	Amount	Unit cost	Quantity	Amount	Quantity	Amount

DISTRIBUTION OF EXPENSES

Month of: _____

Sheet: _____ of _____ 19___

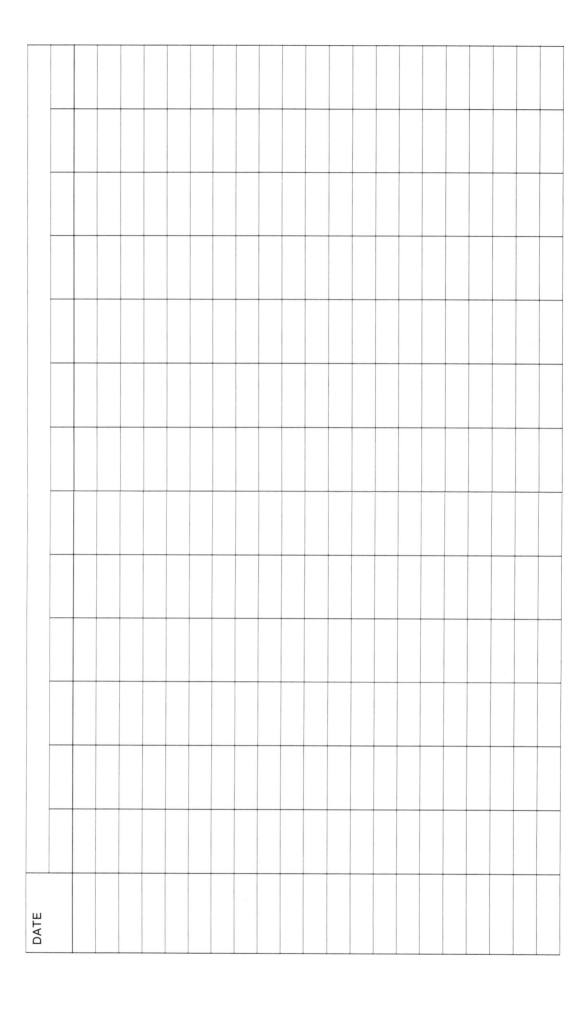

DATE													

REMITTANCE STATEMENT

Date: _____

To:

Your invoice no.	Date	Amount	DEDUCTIONS Date	Description	Amount	Discount	Total

NET PAYABLE [   ]

Requested by: _____

Approved by: _____

Charge to: _____

REMITTANCE STATEMENT

Date: _____

To:

Your invoice no.	Date	Amount	DEDUCTIONS Date	Description	Amount	Discount	Total

NET PAYABLE [   ]

Requested by: _____

Approved by: _____

Charge to: _____

CERTIFICATE OF RESALE

To: _____

_____
(Vendor)

The undersigned hereby certifies that all tangible personal property hereafter purchased by him/her is for the purpose of resale. Purchaser assumes liability for payment of Retailers Occupation Tax, Service Occupation Tax, or Use Tax with respect to receipts from resale of this property.

This certificate shall be considered part of each transaction between Vendor and Purchaser unless otherwise specified.

Purchaser: _____

Address: _____

City: _____

Date: _____

_____
Signature of Purchaser
or Authorizing Agent:

_____
Certificate of Registration
number of Vendor:

_____
Certificate of Registration
number of Purchaser:

RETURN BOTH CERTIFICATES, EACH PROPERLY FILLED OUT, TO THE VENDOR. ONE IS FOR THE STATE DEPARTMENT OF REVENUE, THE OTHER IS FOR OUR RECORDS.

To: _____

_____
(Vendor)

The undersigned hereby certifies that all tangible personal property hereafter purchased by him/her is for the purpose of resale. Purchaser assumes liability for payment of Retailers Occupation Tax, Service Occupation Tax, or Use Tax with respect to receipts from resale of this property.

This certificate shall be considered part of each transaction between Vendor and Purchaser unless otherwise specified.

Purchaser: _____

Address: _____

City: _____

Date: _____

_____
Signature of Purchaser
or Authorizing Agent:

_____
Certificate of Registration
number of Vendor:

_____
Certificate of Registration
number of Purchaser:

EARNINGS STATEMENT

Employee:

Number:

Social Security number:

Period from:

to:

PAYMENTS	# HOURS	RATE	TOTAL
Regular hours:			
Overtime hours:			
Vacation:			
		TOTAL EARNED	

DEDUCTIONS

Social Security (FICA):		
Federal withholding tax:		
State withholding tax:		
Local withholding tax:		
	TOTAL DEDUCTIONS	
	TOTAL NET PAY	

KEEP THIS RECORD OF YOUR EARNINGS

EARNINGS STATEMENT

Employee:

Number:

Social Security number:

Period from:

to:

PAYMENTS	# HOURS	RATE	TOTAL
Regular hours:			
Overtime hours:			
Vacation:			
		TOTAL EARNED	

DEDUCTIONS

Social Security (FICA):		
Federal withholding tax:		
State withholding tax:		
Local withholding tax:		
	TOTAL DEDUCTIONS	
	TOTAL NET PAY	

KEEP THIS RECORD OF YOUR EARNINGS

EARNINGS STATEMENT

Employee:

Number:

Social Security number:

Period from:

to:

PAYMENTS	# HOURS	RATE	TOTAL
Regular hours:			
Overtime hours:			
Vacation:			
		TOTAL EARNED	

DEDUCTIONS

Social Security (FICA):		
Federal withholding tax:		
State withholding tax:		
Local withholding tax:		
	TOTAL DEDUCTIONS	
	TOTAL NET PAY	

KEEP THIS RECORD OF YOUR EARNINGS

EARNINGS STATEMENT

Employee:

Number:

Social Security number:

Period from:

to:

PAYMENTS	# HOURS	RATE	TOTAL
Regular hours:			
Overtime hours:			
Vacation:			
		TOTAL EARNED	

DEDUCTIONS

Social Security (FICA):		
Federal withholding tax:		
State withholding tax:		
Local withholding tax:		
	TOTAL DEDUCTIONS	
	TOTAL NET PAY	

KEEP THIS RECORD OF YOUR EARNINGS

Name: Employee number: Address:

Position: Employment date:

WEEK ENDED	HOURS									RATE	WAGES		TOTAL WAGES
	Sun	Mon	Tue	Wed	Thu	Fri	Sat	Regular	Overtime		Regular	Overtime	
1st Quarter							TOTALS						
2nd Quarter							TOTALS						
3rd Quarter							TOTALS						
4th Quarter							TOTALS						
YEAR							TOTALS						

PAYROLL RECORD, INDIVIDUAL

Social Security number: Number of exemptions: ☐ Single   ☐ Married

DEDUCTIONS							NET PAY	CHECK NUMBER
Social Security	Withholding taxes			Insurance				
	Federal	State	Local					

continued from previous page **PAYROLL RECORD, INDIVIDUAL** 67

PERIOD PAYROLL RECORD

Period from:

to:

NAME	NUMBER OF EXEMPTIONS	HOURS		RATE	WAGES		TOTAL WAGES
		Regular	Overtime		Regular	Overtime	
TOTAL							

THE INSTANT BUSINESS FORMS BOOK

RECORD OF MONTHLY DEPOSITARY PAYMENTS

	January	February	March	
Number of employees:				
Total wages paid:				
Withholding tax:				
Employer's Social Security contribution:				TOTAL
Employees' Social Security contribution:				FOR QUARTER
TOTAL DEPOSIT				

	April	May	June	
Number of employees:				
Total wages paid:				
Withholding tax:				
Employer's Social Security contribution:				TOTAL
Employees' Social Security contribution:				FOR QUARTER
TOTAL DEPOSIT				

	July	August	September	
Number of employees:				
Total wages paid:				
Withholding tax:				
Employer's Social Security contribution:				TOTAL
Employees' Social Security contribution:				FOR QUARTER
TOTAL DEPOSIT				

	October	November	December	
Number of employees:				
Total wages paid:				
Withholding tax:				
Employer's Social Security contribution:				TOTAL
Employees' Social Security contribution:				FOR QUARTER
TOTAL DEPOSIT				

TOTAL FOR YEAR

EXPENSE REPORT WEEKLY

Name: _____

Period from: _____

to: _____

ATTACH RECEIPTS FOR ALL EXPENDITURES

						PERIOD TOTAL
DAY:						
LOCATION:						
LODGING:						
MEALS Breakfast:						
Lunch:						
Dinner:						
TRANSPORTATION LONG DISTANCE Air:						
Rail:						
Bus:						
TRANSPORTATION LOCAL Taxi:						
Bus:						
Auto rental:						
AUTO EXPENSES miles @ ¢:						
Item: (Specify: gas, oil, etc.)						
PARKING:						
TOLLS:						
DAILY TOTAL						TOTAL

ATTACH TO TRAVEL EXPENSE SHEET

	PERIOD TOTAL
TELEPHONE:	
POSTAGE:	
MISCELLANEOUS Itemize:	
DAILY TOTAL	TOTAL

ENTERTAINMENT

Date	Function	Location	Purpose	Name and Title and Company	AMOUNT
					TOTAL

SUBMIT ONLY BUSINESS-RELATED EXPENSES
Number of days business-related travel:
Number of days personal travel:

TOTAL EXPENSES

LESS ADVANCE

BALANCE DUE

ATTACH RECEIPTS FOR ALL EXPENDITURES

Remarks:

Submitted by:

Date:

Approved by:

Date:

EXPENSE REPORT

Month:

Name:

DATE	ITEM	TRAVEL	LODGING	MEALS	MISC	DAILY TOTAL

TOTAL DUE

ATTACH RECEIPTS FOR ALL EXPENDITURES

REQUEST FOR CHECK

Date:

Requested by:

Address:

Reason for check:

Amount requested:

Charge account number:

Amount approved:

Check number:

Approved by:

Received by:

Title:

Date:

REQUEST FOR CHECK

Date:

Requested by:

Address:

Reason for check:

Amount requested:

Charge account number:

Amount approved:

Check number:

Approved by:

Received by:

Title:

Date:

REQUEST FOR ADVANCE

Date:

Requested by:

Address:

Amount requested:

Charge account number:

Amount approved:

Check number:

Reason for advance:

Approved by:

Received by:

Title:

Date:

REQUEST FOR ADVANCE

Date:

Requested by:

Address:

Amount requested:

Charge account number:

Amount approved:

Check number:

Reason for advance:

Approved by:

Received by:

Title:

Date:

PETTY CASH VOUCHER

Number: _____

Date: _____

For

Amount

TOTAL	

Charge account: _____

Approved: _____

Received: _____

PETTY CASH VOUCHER

Number: _____

Date: _____

For

Amount

TOTAL	

Charge account: _____

Approved: _____

Received: _____

PETTY CASH VOUCHER

Number: _____

Date: _____

For

Amount

TOTAL	

Charge account: _____

Approved: _____

Received: _____

PETTY CASH VOUCHER

Number: _____

Date: _____

For

Amount

TOTAL	

Charge account: _____

Approved: _____

Received: _____

PETTY CASH RECONCILIATION

Period from:

to:

Department:

BALANCE
ON HAND

Date	Petty cash voucher no.	Paid to	Charge account no.	Approved by	Total	Balance

TOTAL
VOUCHERS

PETTY CASH
REIMBURSEMENT

BALANCE
BROUGHT FORWARD

Audited by:

Date:

Overage/Shortage:

Approved by:

Date:

CASH DISBURSEMENTS

Period from:

to:

Date	To	For	Charge account	Amount

Audited by:

Date:

Approved by:

Date:

RECEIPT

Receipt number: _____

Received from: _____

For: _____

_____ dollars

ACCOUNT TOTAL _____

THIS PAYMENT _____

BALANCE DUE [_____]

Date: _____

Signed: _____

RECEIPT

Receipt number: _____

Received from: _____

For: _____

_____ dollars

ACCOUNT TOTAL _____

THIS PAYMENT _____

BALANCE DUE [_____]

Date: _____

Signed: _____

RECEIPT

Receipt number: _____

Received from: _____

For: _____

_____ dollars

ACCOUNT TOTAL _____

THIS PAYMENT _____

BALANCE DUE [_____]

Date: _____

Signed: _____

RECEIPT

Receipt number: _____

Received from: _____

For: _____

_____ dollars

ACCOUNT TOTAL _____

THIS PAYMENT _____

BALANCE DUE [_____]

Date: _____

Signed: _____

CASHIER'S VOUCHER

Number: _____

Date: _____

Pay: _____ dollars

_____

Account: _____

Item: _____

Requested by: _____

Approved by: _____

Date: _____

Received by: _____

CASHIER'S VOUCHER

Number: _____

Date: _____

Pay: _____ dollars

_____

Account: _____

Item: _____

Requested by: _____

Approved by: _____

Date: _____

Received by: _____

CASHIER'S VOUCHER

Number: _____

Date: _____

Pay: _____ dollars

_____

Account: _____

Item: _____

Requested by: _____

Approved by: _____

Date: _____

Received by: _____

CASHIER'S VOUCHER

Number: _____

Date: _____

Pay: _____ dollars

_____

Account: _____

Item: _____

Requested by: _____

Approved by: _____

Date: _____

Received by: _____

ACCOUNTS PAYABLE VOUCHER

Voucher number:

Check number:

Date paid:

Payable to:

Audited:

Approved:

Date:

Remarks:

Date	Account number	Amount

TOTAL

DISCOUNT

NET

ACCOUNTS PAYABLE VOUCHER

Voucher number:

Check number:

Date paid:

Payable to:

Audited:

Approved:

Date:

Remarks:

Date	Account number	Amount

TOTAL

DISCOUNT

NET

OPERA NG EXPENSE FORECAST

F____r beginning: _____
Date: _____
____epared by: _____
_____roved by: _____

EXPENSE		ACTUAL this year	ESTIMATE coming year	DIFFERENCE
PERSONNEL EXPENSES (Salaries, wages, bonuses)	Office:			
	Store:			
	Salespeople:			
	All other:			
	TOTAL			
OPERATING EXPENSES	Advertising:			
	Bad debts:			
	Cash discounts allowed:			
	Delivery:			
	Depreciation:			
	Donations:			
	Dues and subscriptions:			
	Employee benefits:			
	Insurance:			
	Interest:			
	Legal and auditing:			
	Maintenance and repairs:			
	Office supplies:			
	Outboard freight:			
	Postage:			
	Rent or mortgage:			
	Sales expenses:			
	Shipping and storage:			
	Taxes:			
	Telephone:			
	Utilities:			
	Other:			
	TOTAL			
	TOTAL FOR YEAR			

CASH FLOW FORECAST

Date: _____
Prepared by: _____
Approved by: _____

	Estimate	Actual	Estimate	Actual	Estimate	Actual
Cash balance beginning of period:						
Accounts receivable:						
TOTAL CASH AVAILABLE						
DISBURSEMENTS						
Trade payables:						
Payroll:						
General expenses:						
Selling expenses:						
Capital additions:						
Income taxes, total:						
Bank loan payments:						
TOTAL DISBURSEMENTS						
Cash balance end of period:						
Less minimum balances:						
ESTIMATED CASH AVAILABLE						

MONTHLY EXPENSE BUDGET

Month of:

	ESTIMATE	ACTUAL	DIFFERENCE $	%
PERSONNEL Office:				
Store:				
Salespeople:				
Others (List):				
OPERATING Advertising:				
Bad debts:				
Cash discounts:				
Delivery costs:				
Depreciation:				
Dues and subscriptions:				
Employee benefits:				
Insurance:				
Interest:				
Legal and auditing:				
Maintenance and repairs:				
Office supplies:				
Postage:				
Rent or mortgage:				
Sales expenses:				
Shipping and storage:				
Supplies:				
Taxes:				
Telephone:				
Utilities:				
Other (List):				
TOTAL				

YEARLY EXPENSE BUDGET

		ESTIMATE	ACTUAL	DIFFERENCE $	%
PERSONNEL	Office:				
	Store:				
	Salespeople:				
	Others (List):				
OPERATING	Advertising:				
	Bad debts:				
	Cash discounts:				
	Delivery costs:				
	Depreciation:				
	Dues and subscriptions:				
	Employee benefits:				
	Insurance:				
	Interest:				
	Legal and auditing:				
	Maintenance and repairs:				
	Office supplies:				
	Postage:				
	Rent or mortgage:				
	Sales expenses:				
	Shipping and storage:				
	Supplies:				
	Taxes:				
	Telephone:				
	Utilities:				
	Other (List):				
	TOTAL				

FIXED ASSETS DEPRECIATION TABLE

Prepared by:

Date:

	Date of purchase	Item	Total cost	Number years useful lifetime	Salvage value	Total depreciation	Annual depreciation	Depreciation years	
								From	To
1									
2									
3									
4									
5									
6									
7									
8									
9									
10									
11									
12									
13									
14									
15									
16									
17									
18									
19									
20									

TOTAL
ANNUAL FIXED ASSETS
DEPRECIATION

PROFIT & LOSS ANNUAL

Fiscal year ended:

	YEAR % of sales	PREVIOUS YEAR % of sales
Gross sales:		
Less discounts:		
TOTAL NET SALES		
LESS Cost of goods sold:		
Raw materials:		
Labor:		
Overhead:		
TOTAL		
GROSS PROFIT		
LESS Operating expenses:		
Interest:		
TOTAL EXPENSES		
PRETAX PROFIT		

Remarks:

PROFIT & LOSS MONTHLY

Month: _____

	MONTH % of sales	PREVIOUS MONTH % of sales
Gross sales:		
Less discounts:		
TOTAL NET SALES		
LESS Cost of goods sold:		
Raw materials:		
Labor:		
Overhead:		
TOTAL		
GROSS PROFIT		
LESS Operating expenses:		
Interest:		
TOTAL EXPENSES		
PRETAX PROFIT		

Remarks:

YEAR END BALANCE SHEET

Fiscal year ending:

Date:

ASSETS

CURRENT ASSETS

Cash on hand:

Cash in bank:

Inventory:

Accounts receivable:

TOTAL
CURRENT ASSETS

FIXED ASSETS

Real estate, land:

Real estate, buildings:

Original cost:

Less reserve for depreciation:

Furniture and fixtures:

Original cost:

Less reserve for depreciation:

Motor vehicles, machinery:

Original cost:

Less reserve for depreciation:

TOTAL
FIXED ASSETS

TOTAL
ASSETS

LIABILITIES

CURRENT LIABILITIES

Accounts payable:

Notes payable:

Taxes payable:

TOTAL
CURRENT
LIABILITIES

NET
WORTH

PERSONAL FINANCIAL STATEMENT

Date: _____

Name: _____
Address:

Telephone: _____

To procure and maintain credit with the above firm, the undersigned submits the following as a true and accurate statement of financial condition on this date. The undersigned will immediately notify said firm of any change that materially reduces the means or ability of the undersigned to pay any claim. Unless the firm is so notified it may continue to rely upon the statement herein given as a true and accurate financial statement of the undersigned.

Signed: _____   Date: _____

ASSETS	AMOUNT	LIABILITIES	AMOUNT
Cash on hand:	_____	Notes payable:	_____
Cash in bank:	_____	Secured:	_____
Branch:		Unsecured:	_____
Account number:		Accounts payable:	_____
Type of account:		Taxes and interest payable:	_____
bank:	_____	Mortgages payable:	_____
Branch:		Liens payable:	_____
Account number:		OTHER DEBTS (Itemize)	_____
Type of account:			_____
Securities:	_____		_____
Accounts and notes receivable:	_____		_____
Real estate owned:	_____		_____
Real estate mortgaged:	_____		_____
Motor vehicles:	_____		_____
Personal property:	_____		_____
OTHER ASSETS (Itemize)	_____		_____
	_____		_____
	_____		_____
	_____		_____
TOTAL ASSETS		**TOTAL LIABILITIES**	

INCOME	AMOUNT		
Specify:	_____		
	_____		
	_____		
TOTAL INCOME		**NET WORTH**	

PERSONAL FINANCIAL WORKSHEET

Date: _____

SCHEDULE OF STOCKS AND BONDS OWNED

Description	In name of	Market value	Maturity

SCHEDULE OF REAL ESTATE OWNED

Description	Date acquired	Title in name of	Cost	Market value	Mortgage amount	Maturity date

SCHEDULE OF MORTGAGES OWNED

Description	Date acquired	In name of	Maturity	Amount

SCHEDULE OF LIFE INSURANCE

Name of company	Beneficiary	Amount	Cash surrender value	Loans against

BANKS OR FINANCIAL INSTITUTIONS WHERE CREDIT HAS BEEN OBTAINED

Name	Address	High credit	Current collateral

Signature: _____

DAILY PLANNER

Day:

Date:

Time	
6:00	
6:30	
7:00	
7:30	
8:00	
8:30	
9:00	
9:30	
10:00	
10:30	
11:00	
11:30	
12:00	
12:30	
1:00	
1:30	
2:00	
2:30	
3:00	
3:30	
4:00	
4:30	
5:00	
5:30	
6:00	
6:30	
7:00	
7:30	
8:00	
8:30	
9:00	

Remarks:

WEEKLY PLANNER

Week beginning:

through:

Time	Monday	Tuesday	Wednesday	Thursday	Friday	Saturday	Sunday
6:00							
6:30							
7:00							
7:30							
8:00							
8:30							
9:00							
9:30							
10:00							
10:30							
11:00							
11:30							
12:00							
12:30							
1:00							
1:30							
2:00							
2:30							
3:00							
3:30							
4:00							
4:30							
5:00							
5:30							
6:00							
6:30							
7:00							
7:30							
8:00							

Remarks:

MONTHLY PLANNER

Month of:

1	
2	
3	
4	
5	
6	
7	
8	
9	
10	
11	
12	
13	
14	
15	
16	
17	
18	
19	
20	
21	
22	
23	
24	
25	
26	
27	
28	
29	
30	
31	

Remarks:

	January	February	March	April	May	June
1						
2						
3						
4						
5						
6						
7						
8						
9						
10						
11						
12						
13						
14						
15						
16						
17						
18						
19						
20						
21						
22						
23						
24						
25						
26						
27						
28						
29						
30						
31						

Remarks:

YEARLY PLANNER

Year beginning:

through:

July	August	September	October	November	December

DAILY SHIPPING REPORT

Reporting period from:

to:

Date:

Page: _____ of _____ pages

Initials	Time	Shipped to	Order number	Description	Shipped via	Shipped to address	Zone	Number of cartons	Weight

Approved by: _____

Date: _____

PACKING SLIP

Date:

Your order number:

Our order number:

Date:

Sold to:

Ship to:

Quantity ordered	Item number	Description	Quantity shipped	Number of cartons	Weight

Packed by:

Balance to ship:

PACKING SLIP

Date:

Your order number:

Our order number:

Date:

Sold to:

Ship to:

Quantity ordered	Item number	Description	Quantity shipped	Number of cartons	Weight

Packed by:

Balance to ship:

PURCHASE ORDER LOG

Purchase order number	Date	Issued to	For	Due	Total amount

PURCHASE ORDER

Purchase order number: _____

Date: _____

⌐To: ¬ ⌐Ship to: ¬

└   ┘ └   ┘

PACKING INSTRUCTION   Attention of: _____
Mark cartons: _____ Deliver by: ____
                                       Ship via:
_____   ☐ UPS   ☐ Parcel post   ☐ Common
Bill to: ☐ Air freight ☐ Other   carrier

_____   Comments: _____
Attention of: _____
INCLUDE OUR PURCHASE ORDER NUMBER   _____
ON ALL DOCUMENTS   Freight charges: ☐ Prepaid   ☐ Collect

If undeliverable: Terms:
☐ Backorder   ☐ Substitute (specify)   ☐ COD   ☐ 1/10 EOM   ☐ Other
☐ Cancel   ☐ Notify   ☐ Net 30 ☐ 2/10 EOM

	Quantity	Item no.	Description		Unit price	Amount
1						
2						
3						
4						
5						
6						
7						
8						
9						
10						

TOTAL ITEMS ORDERED

TOTAL COST ☐

Special instructions: _____

Signed: _____

Date: _____

PURCHASE ORDER

Purchase order
number:

Date:

To:

Ship to:

Ship via:

Deliver on
or before:

Terms:

Quantity	Description	Unit cost	Amount

TOTAL

Special Instructions:

PURCHASE ORDER

Purchase order
number:

Date:

To:

Ship to:

Ship via:

Deliver on
or before:

Terms:

Quantity	Description	Unit cost	Amount

TOTAL

Special Instructions:

RECEIVING REPORT

Date: _____

Our order number: _____

Freight bill number: _____

Received from: _____

Address: _____

Shipped via:

☐ Air ☐ UPS ☐ Parcel post

☐ Prepaid ☐ Collect $ _____

☐ Complete ☐ Partial

Number of cartons: _____ Weight: _____

Quantity	Description	Stock number

☐ Accepted ☐ Reship (date)

☐ Returned ☐ Cancel

Condition: _____

Received by: _____

MEMO

To: _____

From: _____

Date: _____

Re: _____

MEMO

To: _____

From: _____

Date: _____

Re: _____

MEMO

To: _____

From: _____

Date: _____

Re: _____

FAX TRANSMITTAL

TO: _____

COMPANY: _____

PHONE NO: _____ FAX NO: _____

DATE: _____

FROM: _____ DEPT: _____

COMPANY: _____

PHONE NO: _____ FAX NO: _____

REGARDING: _____

_____

_____

_____

_____

_____

NUMBER OF PAGES SENT (Including Cover Sheet): _____

FAX COVER SHEET

TO: _____   FROM: _____

COMPANY: _____   COMPANY: _____

FAX NO: _____   OUR FAX NO: _____

PHONE NO: _____   OUR PHONE NO: _____

NO. OF PAGES (INCLUDING COVER): _____   DATE: _____

RE: _____

_____

_____

_____

_____

_____

_____

_____

_____

_____

_____

ITINERARY

For (day/week): _____

Date: _____

Name: _____

Location: _____

Call	Item	Result	Reschedule
1 Name: Address:			
2 Name: Address:			
3 Name: Address:			
4 Name: Address:			
5 Name: Address:			
6 Name: Address:			
7 Name: Address:			

Remarks:

TIMETABLE

Date: _____

Week from: _____

to: _____

Name	Monday	Tuesday	Wednesday	Thursday	Friday	Saturday	Sunday

VACATION SCHEDULE

NAME	VACATION EARNED	Month																																
		MAY							JUNE							JULY																			

	AUGUST									SEPTEMBER									OTHER										

DAILY APPOINTMENT RECORD

Name: _____

Date: _____

Location: _____

Time record for: _____

Client	Service	Scheduled appointment	Time started	Time stopped	Total time	Next appointment

TOTAL
NUMBER OF APPOINTMENTS [   ]

TOTAL
TIME [   ]

EDUCATION

	NAME AND LOCATION	TYPE OF DIPLOMA	DATES ATTENDED	DID YOU GRADUATE?
HIGH SCHOOL				
TRADE OR TECHNICAL SCHOOL				
COLLEGE				

List any special skills or training:

IMPORTANT — PLEASE READ AND SIGN

As an 'equal opportunity employer' this company's policy, as well as Federal and State Law, prohibits discrimination in employment based on race, color, religion, sex, national origin, physical handicap, or age with respect to individuals who are at least 18 years of age.

As part of this application for employment, I hereby authorize the company to investigate my references and to make an independent investigation of my character, conduct and employment records.

I further agree that failure to reveal any prior employer, or the giving of false or misleading information by me will be grounds for termination of employment.

Signature:

Date:

FOR COMPANY USE ONLY

Interviewer

Date:

Comments:

HIRED

Department:

Position:

Starting date:

Location:

Salary:

Approved:

EMPLOYEE TIMESHEET

Name: _____

Period from: _____

to: _____

Employee number: _____

Position: _____

DATE	AM			PM			OVERTIME			TOTAL HOURS	
	In	Out	Number of hours	In	Out	Number of hours	In	Out	Number of hours	Regular	Overtime

Reason for absence: _____

Signed: _____

Approved: _____

ROUTING SLIP

Date:

ROUTE TO

When finished, cross out your name
and pass on.

ROUTING SLIP

Date:

ROUTE TO

When finished, cross out your name
and pass on.

ROUTING SLIP

Date:

ROUTE TO

When finished, cross out your name
and pass on.

ROUTING SLIP

Date:

ROUTE TO

When finished, cross out your name
and pass on.

LONG DISTANCE CALL RECORD

Placed by: For:

Call to: Title:

Telephone number: Area code:

Company and address:

Zip:

Subject of call/result:

Date: Time:

☐ Person to person   ☐ Paid
☐ Station to station   Charge to:
☐ Collect

LONG DISTANCE CALL RECORD

Placed by: For:

Call to: Title:

Telephone number: Area code:

Company and address:

Zip:

Subject of call/result:

Date: Time:

☐ Person to person   ☐ Paid
☐ Station to station   Charge to:
☐ Collect

LONG DISTANCE CALL RECORD

Placed by: For:

Call to: Title:

Telephone number: Area code:

Company and address:

Zip:

Subject of call/result:

Date: Time:

☐ Person to person   ☐ Paid
☐ Station to station   Charge to:
☐ Collect

LONG DISTANCE CALL RECORD

Placed by: For:

Call to: Title:

Telephone number: Area code:

Company and address:

Zip:

Subject of call/result:

Date: Time:

☐ Person to person   ☐ Paid
☐ Station to station   Charge to:
☐ Collect

TELEPHONE CALL RECORD

Date	Caller	Call to	Company and address	City	Area code	Telephone number	Charges	Billed

Note:

ADDRESS REFERENCE SHEET

Page number:
_____

Date revised:
_____

Name	Address	Zip code	Area code	Telephone

THE INSTANT BUSINESS FORMS BOOK

INSPECTION REGISTER

Equipment: _____

Location: _____

Date	Time	Remarks	Action	Initials

Date: _____

Signed: _____

WEEKLY MANAGEMENT CHECKLIST

Month:

SOURCE			WEEK:		1	2	3	4	5
(	)	SALES	Last week:	$					
(	)	SALES	Month-to-date:	$					
(	)	SALES This month last year:		$					
(	)	SALES	Year to date:	$					
(	)	SALES	Year-to-date target:	$					
(	)		Promotion projects behind schedule:	#					
(	)		Return on net sales, Year-to-date:	%					
(	)		Projects under consideration:	#					
(	)		Contracted projects in pipeline:	#					
(	)		Transmissions behind schedule:	#					
(	)	New projects in production:		#					
(	)	Reorders in production:		#					
(	)		Production jobs behind schedule:	#					
(	)	Oldest unfilled order:		#					
(	)	Out-of-stock items:		#					
(	)		Items below 3 months supply:	#					
(	)	Cash on hand:		$					
(	)	Working capital position:		$					
(	)	Inventory value:		$					
(	)		Accounts receivable over 90 days:	%					
(	)		Bad debts on net sales, Year-to-date:	%					
(	)		Supply items not in inventory:	#					
(	)		Equipment items not functional	#					

STATE INSPECTION TIME RECORD

Timesheet for week of: _____

to: _____

NAME	EMPLOYEE NUMBER	MONDAY			TUESDAY			WEDNESDAY			THURSDAY			FRIDAY			SATURDAY			SUNDAY			TOTAL HOURS FOR WEEK
		In	Out	Total	In	Out	Total	In	Out	Total	In	Out	Total	In	Out	Total	In	Out	Total	In	Out	Total	

QUOTATION REQUEST

Date:

Job name:

Job number:

To:

JOB DESCRIPTION

REPLY

Estimated time:

Hourly/daily rate:

TOTAL
ESTIMATED
LABOR COST

Estimated cost of materials:

Estimated expenses:

TOTAL
COST

Additional hours/days will be
charged at the rate of $:

Remark:

Based on a schedule of:

Terms and conditions:

Quotation valid until:

Signed:

Date:

QUOTATION REQUEST

Date:

Job number:

To:

Quantity	Item	Unit cost	Total

Schedule of delivery:

Packing and shipping
requirements:

Payment terms:

Quotation valid until:

Signed:

Date:

QUOTATION REQUEST

Date:

Job number:

To:

Quantity	Item	Unit cost	Total

Schedule of delivery:

Packing and shipping requirements:

Payment terms:

Quotation valid until:

Signed:

Date:

QUOTATION REQUEST

Date:

Job number:

To:

Quantity	Item	Unit cost	Total

Schedule of delivery:

Packing and shipping requirements:

Payment terms:

Quotation valid until:

Signed:

Date:

QUOTATION

Date:

Your job number:

Our quotation number:

To:

JOB DESCRIPTION AND SPECIFICATIONS

MATERIALS REQUIRED	Quantity	Description	Unit cost	Amount
			TOTAL MATERIALS COST	

LABOR REQUIRED	Days	Rate	Hours	Rate	Amount
Regular:					
Overtime:					
				TOTAL LABOR COST	
				TOTAL JOB ESTIMATE	

1 Quotation is based on a schedule of:

2 Additional materials and/or labor will be charged accordingly.

3 Terms and conditions:

4 Quotation valid until:

5 Remarks:

Signed:

QUOTATION

Date: _____

Your job number: _____

Our quotation number: _____

To:

Quantity	Item no.	Description	Unit count	Unit price	Amount

TOTAL

Delivery to: _____   Date: _____

Via: _____

FOB: _____

This quotation is valid from: _____

to: _____

Terms and conditions:

Remarks:

Signature: _____

Title: _____

Date: _____

QUOTATION

Date:
Your job no:
Our quotation no:

To:

Quantity	Item no.	Description	Unit count	Unit price	Amount

TOTAL

Delivery to:
Date:
Via:
FOB:

This quotation is valid from:
to:

Terms and conditions:

Remarks:

Signature:
Title:
Date:

QUOTATION

Date:
Your job no:
Our quotation no:

To:

Quantity	Item no.	Description	Unit count	Unit price	Amount

TOTAL

Delivery to:
Date:
Via:
FOB:

This quotation is valid from:
to:

Terms and conditions:

Remarks:

Signature:
Title:
Date:

QUOTATION COMPARISON

Date: _____

Job: _____

Job number: _____

Job description: _____

Firm	Contact	Item	Quantity	Delivery schedule	Terms	Total price	Unit price	Delivery charge	Net price	Remarks

Notes:

INVENTORY

Date: _____

Page number: _____

Department: _____

Location: _____

Priced by: _____   Checked by: _____   Called by: _____   Entered by: _____

Extended by: _____   Checked by: _____   Footed by: _____   Examined by: _____

	Quantity	Unit	Description	Unit price	Extension	Total
1						
2						
3						
4						
5						
6						
7						
8						
9						
10						
11						
12						
13						
14						
15						
16						
17						
18						
19						
20						
21						
22						
23						
24						
25						

TOTAL [   ]

PERPETUAL INVENTORY

Item:

Item number:

Sheet number:

ORDERED

Date	Order number	Quantity	Date due

RECEIVED

Date	Order number	Quantity

SOLD

Date	Order number	Quantity	Balance	Comments

PERPETUAL INVENTORY

Item: _____

Item number: _____

Sheet number: _____

ORDERED			
Date	Order no.	Quantity	Date due

SOLD				
Date	Order no.	Quantity	Balance	Comments

RECEIVED		
Date	Order no.	Quantity

PERPETUAL INVENTORY

Item: _____

Item number: _____

Sheet number: _____

ORDERED			
Date	Order no.	Quantity	Date due

SOLD				
Date	Order no.	Quantity	Balance	Comments

RECEIVED		
Date	Order no.	Quantity

STOCK RECORD CARD

Item: _____   Size: _____
                            Unit: _____

Location: _____   Minimum: _____
                            Maximum: _____

Item number: _____

RECEIVED					RELEASED			BALANCE ON HAND
Initials	Date	Order number	Quantity	Date due	Date	Order number	Quantity	

STOCK RECORD CARD

Item: Size:
                               Unit:

Location: Minimum:
                               Maximum:

Item number:

RECEIVED					RELEASED			BALANCE
Initials	Date	Order number	Quantity	Date due	Date	Order number	Quantity	ON HAND

STOCK RECORD CARD

Item: Size:
                               Unit:

Location: Minimum:
                               Maximum:

Item number:

RECEIVED					RELEASED			BALANCE
Initials	Date	Order number	Quantity	Date due	Date	Order number	Quantity	ON HAND

REQUISITION SLIP

Date: _____

Number _____

From: _____

Charge to: _____

Deliver to: _____

Job number: _____

Attention: _____

Item number	Quantity	Description	Unit of purchase	Unit price	Cost	Date required

Specifications.

Recommended suppliers: _____

TOTAL COST [   ]

Requisitioned by: _____

Date: _____

REQUISITION SLIP

Date: _____

Number _____

From: _____

Charge to: _____

Deliver to: _____

Job number: _____

Attention: _____

Item number	Quantity	Description	Unit of purchase	Unit price	Cost	Date required

Specifications:

Recommended suppliers: _____

TOTAL COST [   ]

Requisitioned by: _____

Date: _____

OUT OF STOCK NOTICE

Date: _____

Your order number: _____

Your order date: _____

To:

Item number	Description	Quantity

Your order cannot be filled because we are temporarily out of stock for the above. Please complete the form below and return to us. We apologize for any inconvenience.

Estimated shipping date: _____

Back order ☐
—ship as soon
as possible

Substitute (specify) ☐

Cancel ☐

Signed: _____

Please return form to:

_____

OUT OF STOCK NOTICE

Date:

Order no:

Your order date:

To:

Item number	Description	Quantity

Your order cannot be filled because we are temporarily out of stock for the above. Please complete the form below and return to us. We apologize for any inconvenience.

Estimated shipping date:

Please return form to:

☐ Back order
— ship as soon as possible

☐ Substitute (specify)

☐ Cancel

Signed:

OUT OF STOCK NOTICE

Date:

Order no:

Your order date:

To:

Item number	Description	Quantity

Your order cannot be filled because we are temporarily out of stock for the above. Please complete the form below and return to us. We apologize for any inconvenience.

Estimated shipping date:

Please return form to:

☐ Back order
—ship as soon as possible

☐ Substitute (specify)

☐ Cancel

Signed:

EMPLOYEE PURCHASE FORM

Name:

Department:

Date:

Quantity	Description	List price	Discount	Employee cost

TOTAL

Approved by:

EMPLOYEE PURCHASE FORM

Name:

Department:

Date:

Quantity	Description	List price	Discount	Employee cost

TOTAL

Approved by:

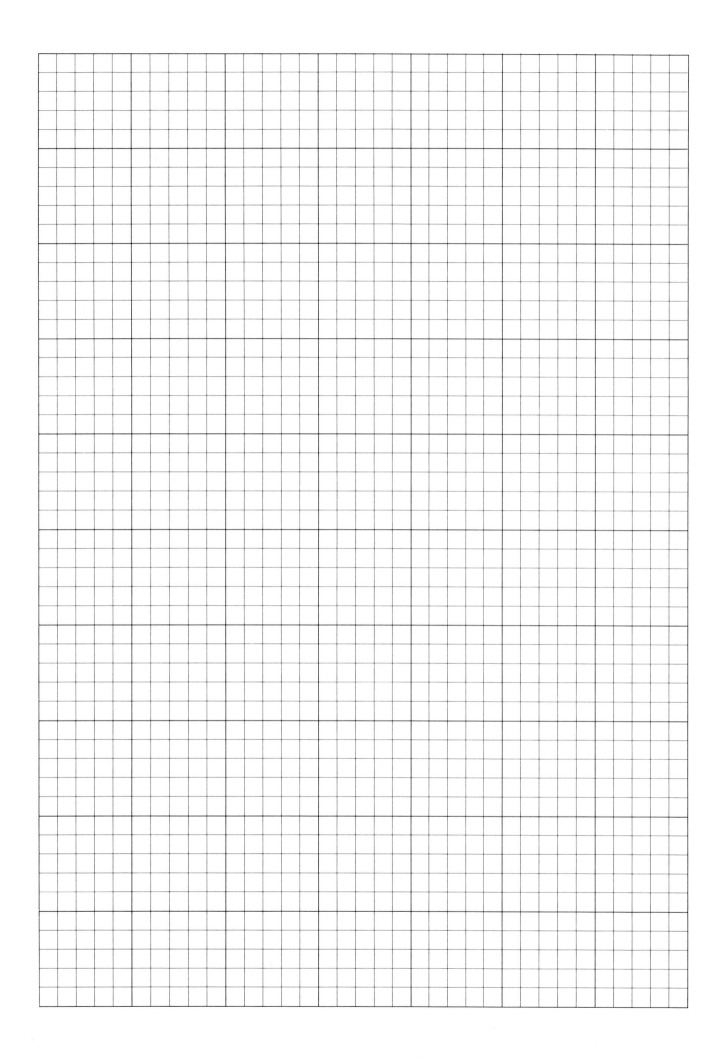

1″ GRID by ⅕″ divisions 153

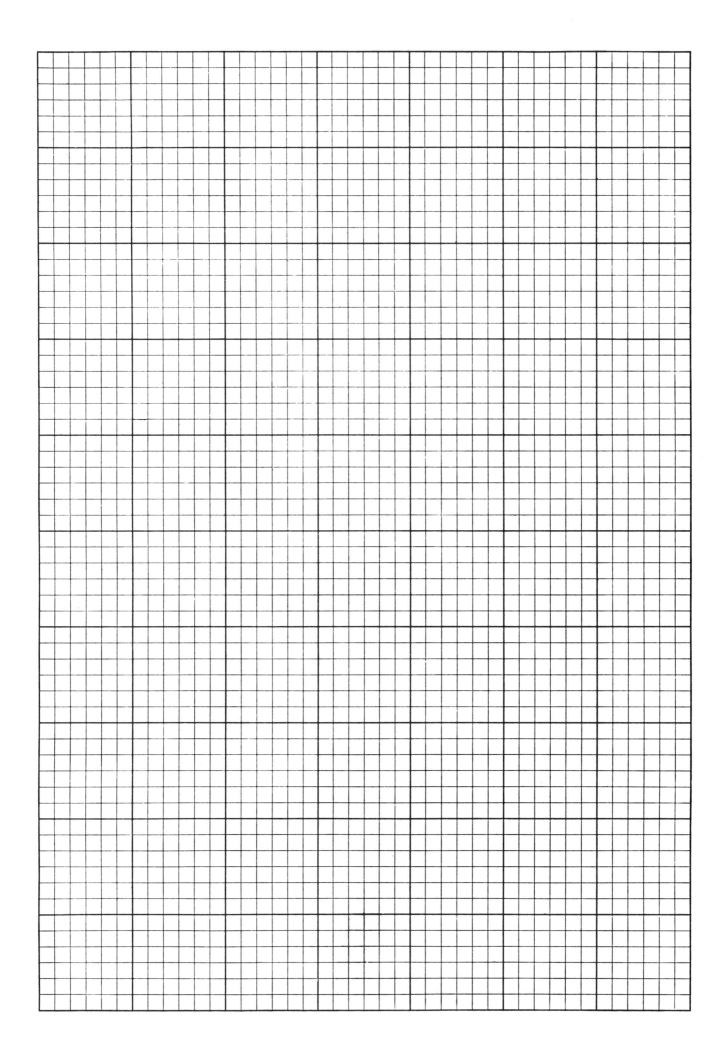

THE INSTANT BUSINESS FORMS BOOK

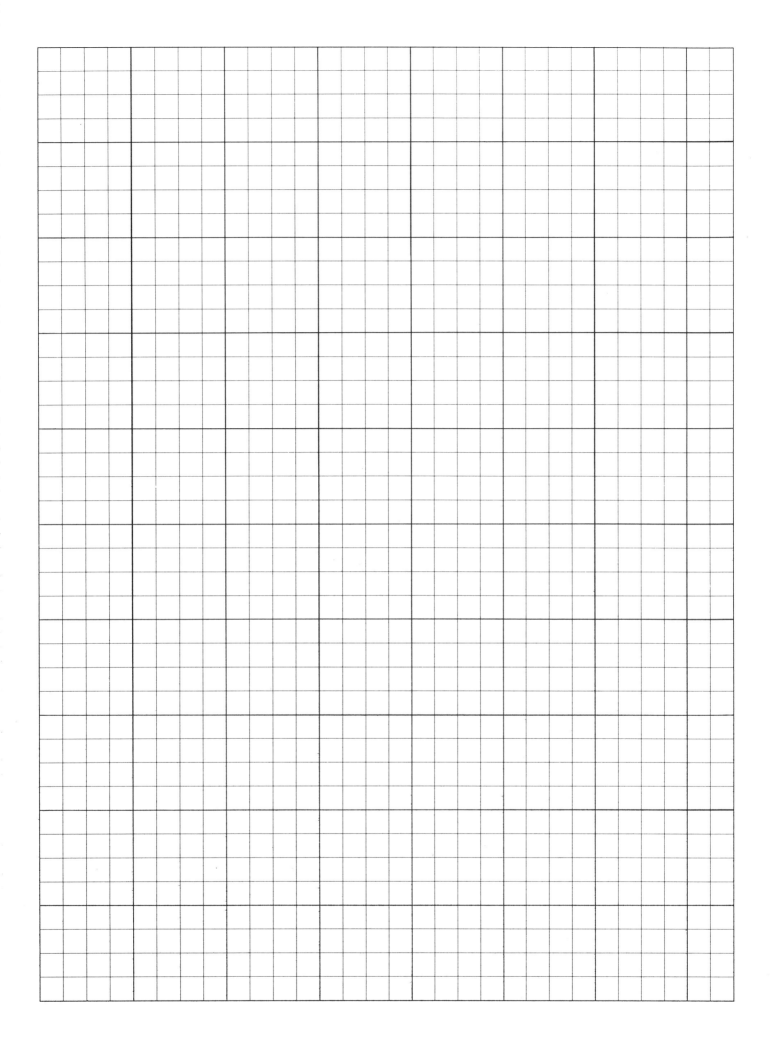

1″ **GRID** by ¼″ divisions 155

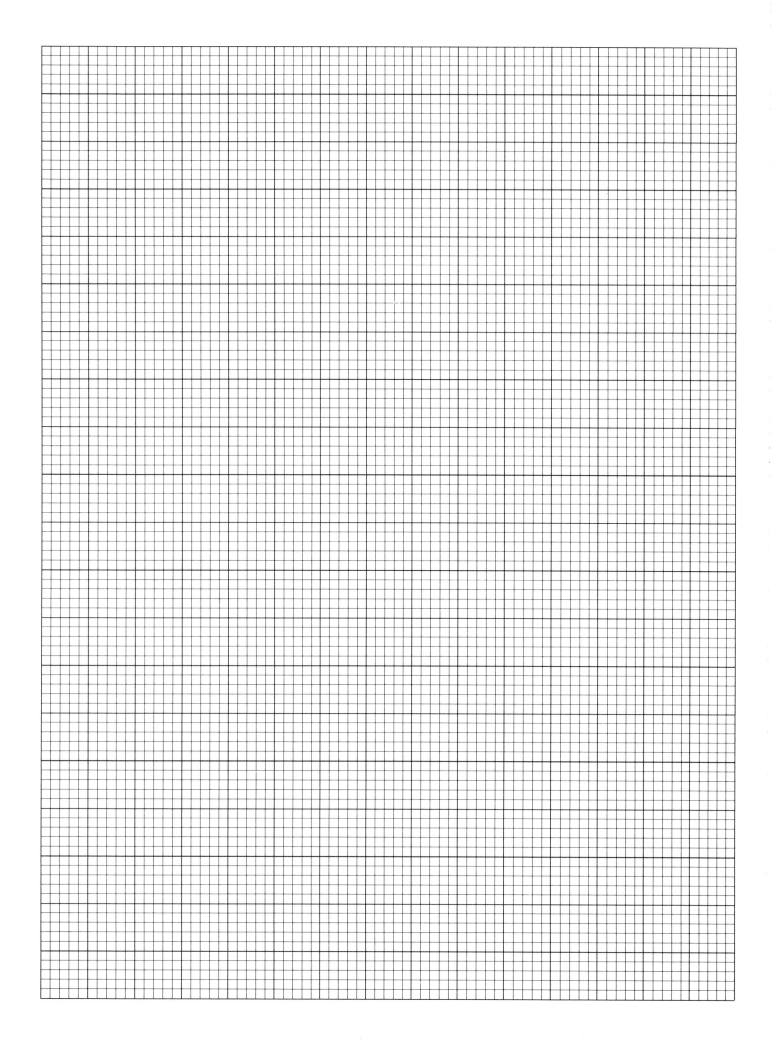

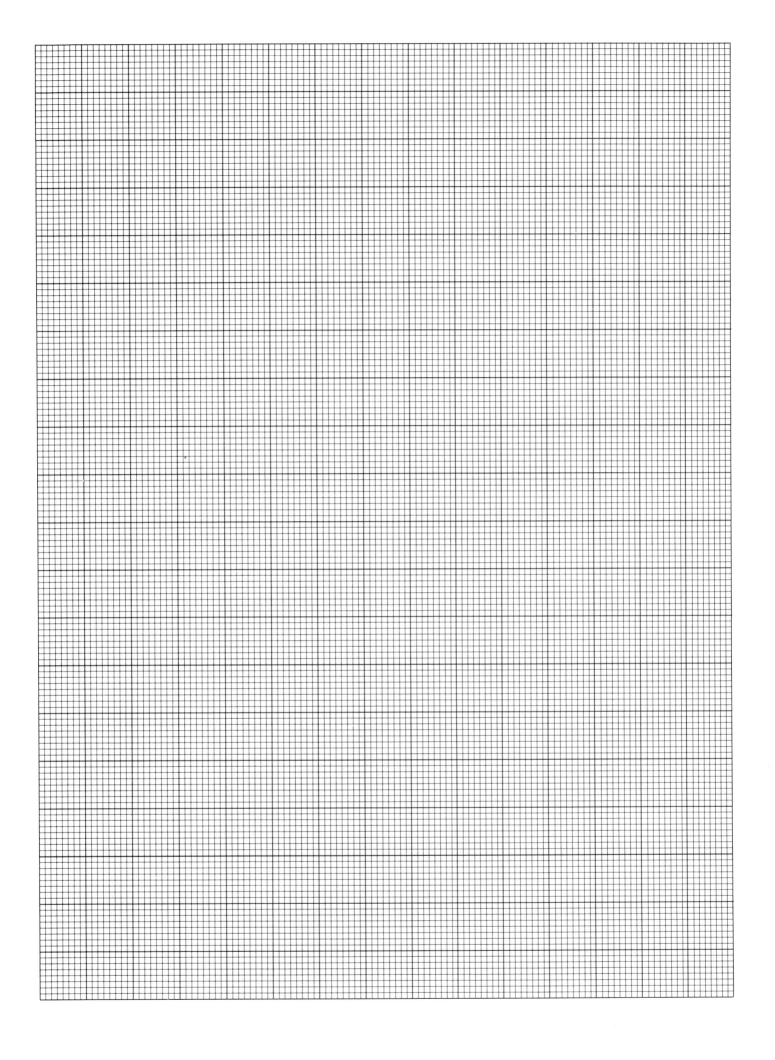

1″ **GRID** by ¹⁄₁₆″ divisions 157
THE INSTANT BUSINESS FORMS BOOK

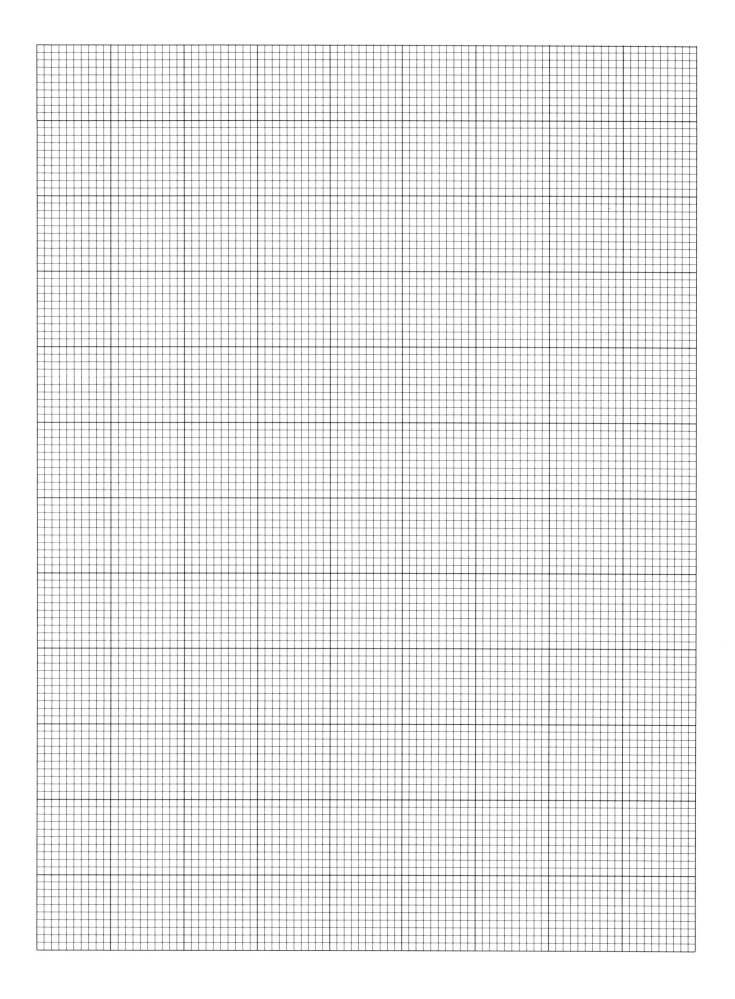

158 GRID by 2mm divisions
THE INSTANT BUSINESS FORMS BOOK

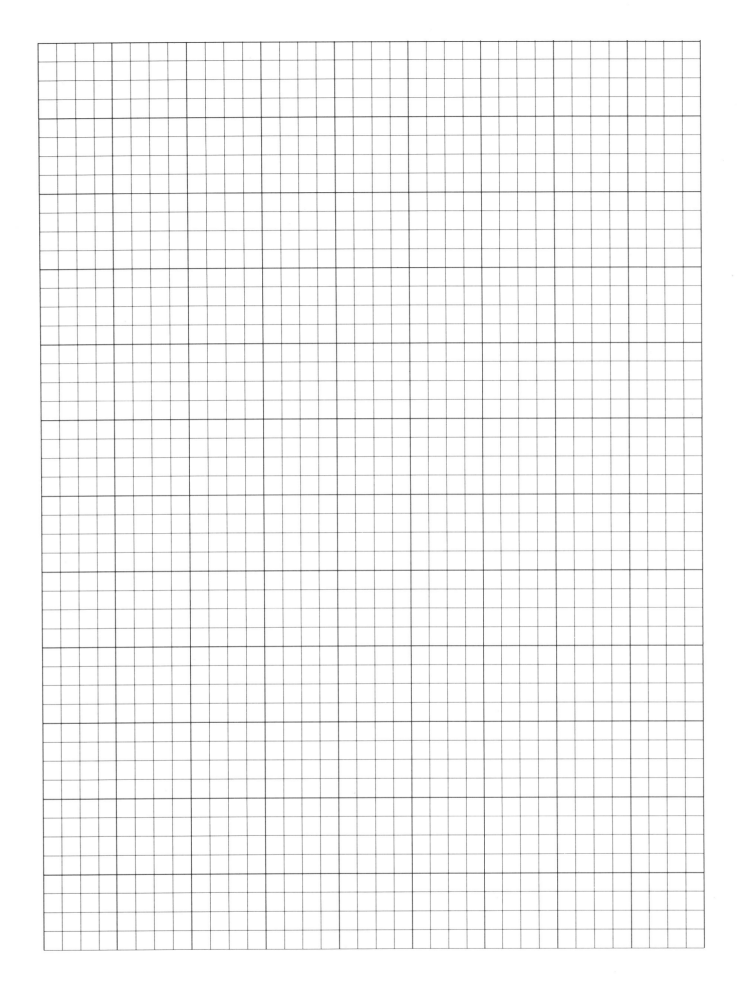